I TOOK A WALK

BY HENRY COLE

Greenwillow Books, New York

To Anne, with whom
I wandered past many
a meandering stream

Acrylic paints were used for the full-color art. The text type is Kabel.
Copyright © 1998 by Henry Cole
All rights reserved. No part of this book may be reproduced or utilized in any form or by
any means, electronic or mechanical, including photocopying, recording, or by any information
storage and retrieval system, without permission in writing from the Publisher, Greenwillow Books,
a division of William Morrow & Company, Inc., 1350 Avenue of the Americas, New York, NY 10019.
http://www.williammorrow.com   Printed in Singapore by Tien Wah Press
First Edition   10   9   8   7   6   5   4   3   2   1

Library of Congress Cataloging-in-Publication Data
Cole, Henry.
I took a walk / by Henry Cole.
p.   cm.
Summary: A visit to woods, pasture, and pond brings encounters
with various birds, insects, and other creatures of nature. Flaps fold
out to reveal the animals on each two-page spread.
ISBN 0-688-15115-9
1. Toy and movable books—Specimens.
[1. Animals—Fiction.   2. Nature—Fiction.
3. Toy and movable books.]   I. Title.
PZ7.C67728Iat   1998   [E]—dc21
97-6692   CIP   AC

One spring morning
I went for a walk
and followed the path
to the woods....

I sat in the cool shade
and poked my head
through the soft ferns.
I saw . . .

I wandered out of the woods and into a meadow.
I wonder who's watching me?

I lay down in the middle of the meadow and smelled the sweet red clover.
I saw...

I found a path that
led to a meandering stream.
I wonder who's watching me?

I sat on the bank
of the stream and
brushed aside the
spicebush leaves.
I saw…

I followed the stream
and came to a pond.
I wonder who's
watching me?

I sat quietly at the edge
of the pond and peered
through the tall cattails.
I saw . . .

Find a place to sit
and watch and listen.
What do you see?

IN THE WOODS

1. a camouflaged fawn
2. an ovenbird
3. an ovenbird's nest
4. fungus on a fallen log
5. a deer antler
6. a zebra butterfly
7. Jack-in-the-pulpits
8. a grouse family
9. a woodpecker
10. a hawk
11. an owl's home
12. a tiger beetle
13. signs of a squirrel
14. a millipede

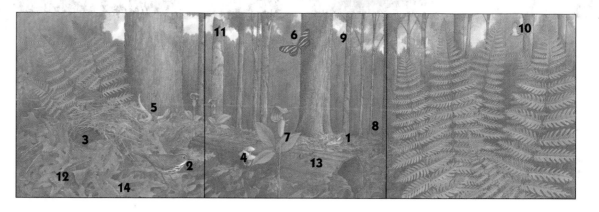

IN THE MEADOW

1. a quail (or bobwhite)
2. the tail of a blacksnake
3. a milkweed beetle
4. a meadowlark's nest
5. a male box turtle
6. a monarch butterfly
7. a grasshopper
8. a wolf spider
9. a butterfly chrysalis
10. a spittlebug's home
11. a skipper butterfly
12. a soldier beetle
13. fireflies
14. oxeye daisies
15. milkweed

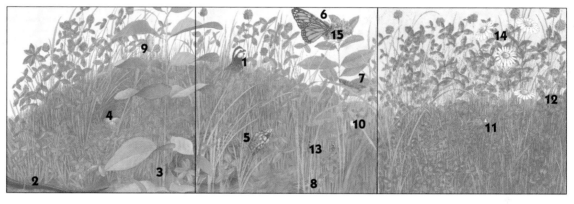

AT THE STREAM

1. bank swallows
2. a bank swallow's nest
3. a green snake
4. a wood duck family
5. a kingfisher
6. a mourning cloak butterfly
7. a mayfly
8. a spicebush butterfly
9. a tiger swallowtail butterfly
10. a paper wasp's nest
11. signs of a beaver
12. deer tracks

AT THE POND

1. a grebe on her nest
2. a heron
3. whirligig beetles
4. a bluegill
5. tree swallows
6. a rail
7. a painted turtle
8. a damselfly
9. a marsh wren's nest
10. yellow iris
11. a dragonfly
12. a minnow
13. water lilies

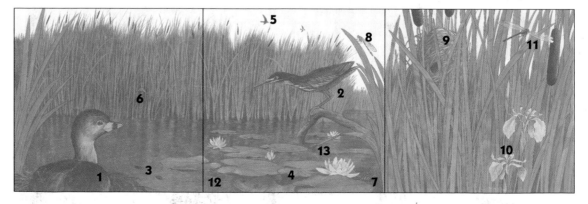